ENGINE STOPS!
SEA START IT.

NIGHT AND DAY WE'RE JUST A CALL AWAY

SO JOIN NOW.

**24 HOURS, 365 DAYS A YEAR
MECHANICAL BREAKDOWN ASSISTANCE**

Marinecall®

WEATHER AT SEA

Accurate. Reliable. Conclusive.
Marinecall, forecasting you can depend on.

DETAILED 5-DAY FORECASTS BY PHONE
09068 500 4
+ area number

48-HOUR FORECASTS WITH SYNOPTIC CHARTS
FAX 09065 300 2
+ area number

Information Supplied by
The Met.Office

Offshore Areas	2-5 Day Planner by Phone 09068 500 +	2-5 Day Planner by Fax 09065 300 +
English Channel	992	270
Southern North Sea	991	271
Irish Sea	954	273
Biscay	953	274
North West Scotland	955	275
Northern North Sea	985	276
Index page to all fax products	-	09068 24 66 80

Marinecall Club
A unique prepaid service providing discounted local 7-Day forecasts available from any telephone, including mobiles.

Marinecall FaxDirect
Discounted forecasts faxed automatically to you on a daily or weekly basis.
For more information contact Marinecall Customer Helpdesk 0870 600 4219

09068 calls cost 60p per min., 09065 calls cost £1.50 per min. Thus plc, EC2A 4PF. Based on Met Office data.
Marinecall Customer Helpdesk 0870 600 4219. Marinecall@let-it-be-thus.com

THE SEAWAY CODE

Seamanship and safety for all leisure craft

Written by James Stevens
RYA Training Manager

The Royal Yachting Association

London: The Stationery Office

ACKNOWLEDGEMENTS

The author and The Stationery Office would like to thank the following for their input, advice and assistance: Ben Ainslie for writing the Foreword, Amy Bruton for typing the manuscript, Nigel Orme for the illustrations, John Goode for his technical input, and The Royal Yachting Association. Many thanks also to Harwich Haven Authority for permission to use their harbour map.

Charts were reproduced from RYA training charts numbers 1 and 2, by permission of the Controller of Her Majesty's Stationery Office and the UK Hydrographic Office.

Applications for reproduction should be made in writing to The Stationery Office Limited, St Crispins, Duke Street, Norwich NR3 1PD.

The information contained in this publication is believed to be correct at the time of manufacture. Whilst care has been taken to ensure that the information is accurate, the publisher can accept no responsibility for any errors or omissions or for changes to the details given.

James Stevens has asserted his moral rights under the Copyright, Designs and Patents Act 1988, to be identified as the author of this work.

A CIP catalogue record for this book is available from the British Library. A Library of Congress CIP catalogue record has been applied for.

First published 2001

ISBN 0117025356

Published by The Stationery Office
and available from:

Tel: 0870 600 5522
Fax: 0870 600 5533
www.thestationeryoffice.com

Printed in England by McCorquodale Confidential Print Limited, Milton Keynes, Bucks. TJ3610 C200 2/01

CONTENTS

FOREWORD

In Britain we are fortunate in having thousands of miles of coastline providing us with great opportunities for recreational boating.

Sailing on the sea can be anything from tranquil to exhilarating but it can be dangerous too, unless you know the ropes. We can use wind and tide to our advantage but without knowledge, a pleasant day's sail may turn into an emergency.

This book, compiled by the RYA, provides useful advice and information whether you race, cruise or just potter about in boats. The more you know, the more you will enjoy the sport.

Ben Ainslie

OLYMPIC GOLD MEDALLIST 2000

This book gives advice and guidance for people taking to the sea in all types of small craft from windsurfers to yachts.

It does not, of course, provide the full story; such a small volume can only provide helpful hints and pointers. The best way to learn is to attend an RYA course, where trained instructors can teach you to handle and navigate your craft safely.

There is no requirement for recreational boat users to hold a Certificate of Competence. The Maritime and Coastguard Agency and the Royal Yachting Association prefer to promote a system of voluntary training. This training attracts 120,000 boat users a year, who understand that it is logical and sensible to find out about the sea before venturing out on it.

RYA – www.rya.org.uk
tel 023 8062 7400

GETTING STARTED

If you are a beginner considering buying a boat, take a course first. RYA recognised schools can teach you every form of boating from windsurfing to offshore yachting. You can find out what type of boating you enjoy and your instructor can give you advice about the most suitable craft. You will also be more competent when you set off.

Yachts

A second-hand yacht should be surveyed before purchase. The surveyor will check:

- Sails in good condition
- Mast in good condition
- Fuel system – no leaks
- Hatches secure
- Gas system – no leaks
- Deck fittings secure
- Steering – no 'play'
- Watertight integrity
- Engine in good condition
- Sea cocks functional
- Rigging secure
- Structural strength and condition of hull

Long-keeled yachts are good for long passages and very bad weather but are slower and generally have less accommodation than those with a fin keel.

TIP:
• Choose a yacht with a diesel engine. Petrol is dangerous below decks.

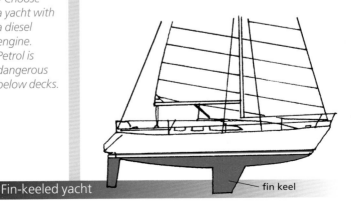

Fin-keeled yacht   fin keel

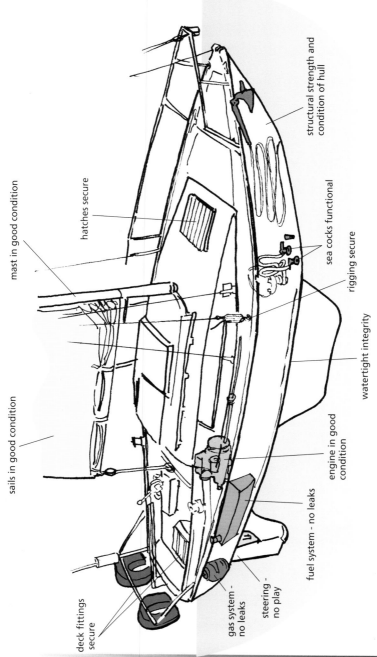

structural strength and
condition of hull

hatches secure

sea cocks functional

mast in good condition

rigging secure

watertight integrity

sails in good condition

engine in good
condition

fuel system - no leaks

deck fittings
secure

gas system -
no leaks

steering -
no play

Motor cruisers

There are two types of transmission:

* Outdrive - Steer by moving the propeller leg
* Fixed propeller - Steer with rudders

They have very different handling characteristics. Outdrives only steer with the power on but they can achieve sharper turns.
For a motor cruiser, choose a surveyor with a good knowledge of engines. Check:

* Secure deck fittings
* Steering and navigation system works efficiently
* Gas system – no leaks
* Windows watertight
* Electrical system works
* Engine
* Fuel system – no leaks

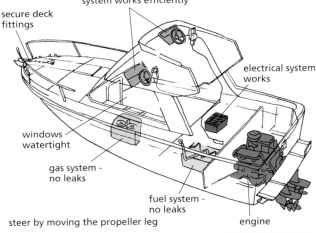

steering and navigation system works efficiently

secure deck fittings

electrical system works

windows watertight

gas system - no leaks

fuel system - no leaks

steer by moving the propeller leg

engine

Outdrive

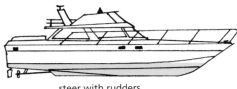

steer with rudders

Fixed propeller

Dinghies

Learn to sail on a stable dinghy. You can move on to the high performance boats later. When purchasing a dinghy check:

- Sails in good condition
- Centreboard case not damaged
- Rudder fitting secure
- Buoyancy tanks undamaged
- Check hull damage
- Rigging secure – no chafe on wires

To check the buoyancy tanks, it is best to deliberately capsize the boat for 10 minutes on each side. There should be no more than about 3 litres in the tank.

TIP:
• *If the dinghy is ashore, pour a few buckets of water in it to check for leaks.*

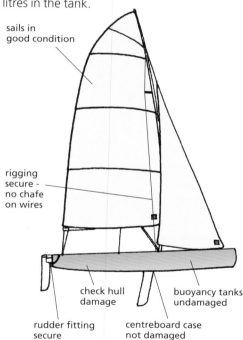

sails in good condition

rigging secure - no chafe on wires

check hull damage

buoyancy tanks undamaged

rudder fitting secure

centreboard case not damaged

Dinghy

Small powerboats

TIP:
• *Keep the boat clear of clutter – cables, fuel tanks and pipes should be stowed tidily.*

When purchasing a small powerboat, check:

- Steering and console secure
- Check seal between inflatable tubes and hard hull
- Cables in good condition
- Kill cord works (stops engine if driver falls out)
- Fuel tanks secure – no leaks
- Outboard serviced and reliable

You need to see the craft in the water to ensure it works efficiently.

steering and console secure

cables in good condition

outboard serviced and reliable

kill cord works (stops engine if driver falls out)

fuel tanks secure - no leaks

check seal between inflatable tubes and hard hull

Small powerboat

Personal watercraft (Jet skis)

TIP:
• *Beware of ropes and stones getting sucked into the jet intake.*

When purchasing, check:

- Kill cord works
- Jets not damaged
- Steering secure
- Engine serviced and reliable
- Fuel system – no leaks
- No leaks into the hull
- Check hull for damage
- Electrics in good condition

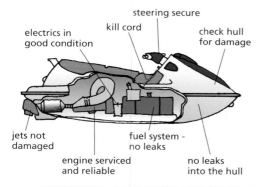

steering secure

kill cord

electrics in
good condition

check hull
for damage

jets not
damaged

fuel system -
no leaks

no leaks
into the hull

engine serviced
and reliable

Personal watercraft

Windsurfers

When purchasing, check:

- Suitable sail in good condition
- Non-slip surface
- Mast not cracked
- Universal joint works and
  is secure on board
- No chafe on boom

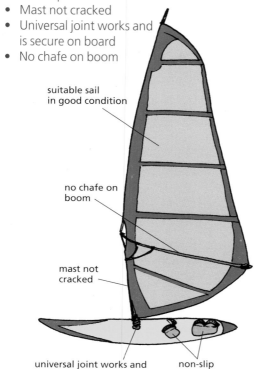

suitable sail
in good condition

no chafe on
boom

TIP:
• *Choose
a sail to
match your
ability.*

mast not
cracked

universal joint works and
is secure on board

non-slip
surface

Windsurfer

EQUIPMENT

Small powerboats and personal watercraft

A small powerboat and personal watercraft should carry:

- A fire extinguisher
- Knife
- Torch for signalling
- Flare pack – with two pinpoint red and two orange smoke
- Folding anchor
- 15 metres of rope for towing and anchoring

Flares

- Basic tool kit and spare spark plugs
- Documentation in a waterproof wallet – some local authorities require proof of insurance and a permit
- Cash – you may end up some way from your car
- First aid kit
- Waterproof hand-held marine VHF radio (licences required for set and operator)

TIP:
• *Keep safety equipment in a sealed waterproof box strapped to the craft.*

ALWAYS WEAR A KILL CORD IN A SMALL POWERBOAT OR PERSONAL WATERCRAFT

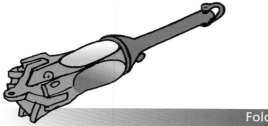

Folding anchor

Dinghies and windsurfers

High performance dinghies and windsurfers cannot practically carry safety equipment and should, therefore, be sailed in sight of a rescue craft or sailed with a buddy system.

AN EXTRA LENGTH OF ROPE FOR REPAIRS AND TOWING IS ESSENTIAL

For cruising, a dinghy should carry:

- Paddles or oars
- Anchor and rope
- Foredeck cleat
- Bailer
- Flares – two pinpoint red and two orange smoke
- Waterproof hand-held marine VHF Radio (licences required for set and operator)
- Laminated chart
- Compass
- Mooring rope
- Waterproof torch
- Spare shackles etc.

TIP:
• A netting attached under the foredeck will keep safety equipment dry.

Compass & VHF radio

Yachts

A yacht's equipment depends on how far offshore you intend to travel.

For offshore passages, the equipment should include:

- Battery, whose sole purpose is to start the engine
- Anchor with at least 10m of chain and warp
  For 7m length craft -
  9kg anchor and 8mm diameter chain and 12mm diameter rope
  For 10m craft -
  13kg anchor and 8mm diameter chain and 12mm diameter rope
- 2 buckets with lanyards
- 2 bilge pumps –
  1 operated from inside the boat with hatches closed and 1 from the cockpit
- Soft wood plugs adjacent to hull fittings
- Sea cocks capable of closing all through hull fittings
- Radar reflector
- Navigation lights
- Sound signal apparatus (foghorn)
- 2 waterproof torches
- Flares -
  4 hand-held pinpoint red
  2 buoyant orange smoke
  4 red parachute rockets
- Fire blanket for craft with cooking equipment
- 2 multi-purpose fire extinguishers sited near the exits to the accommodation, each with a fire rating of 5A/34B
- Large multi-purpose extinguisher 13A/113B
- Automatic or semi-automatic extinguisher in the engine space
- Life-raft capable of carrying all crew
- Grab bag
- 2 horseshoe lifebelts
- 30m buoyant heaving line
- Boarding ladder
- Dan buoy

TIP:

• Keep a grab bag of emergency equipment ready in case you have to abandon the boat.

Radar reflector

- Marine VHF radio
- Emergency hand-held VHF radio
- Emergency VHF aerial
- Radio receiver to receive broadcast shipping forecasts
- Charts, Almanac and navigational publications
- Steering compass, lit at night
- Hand bearing compass
- Navigation instruments
- Barometer
- Echo sounder
- GPS electronic navigation set
- Clock
- Distance measuring log
- Binoculars
- Emergency tiller
- Towing warp
- Mooring warps and fenders
- Spare fuel
- Inflatable dinghy
- Tool kit
- Spares for engine
- Emergency water
- Bosun's chair

TIPS:

• *You can stow life-rafts upright on the stern rail but they have to be specially packed.*

• *Remember charts have to be up-dated – your local chart agent can provide corrections.*

• *The RNLI's sea check service gives advice on equipment for all types of craft. Call them on*

01202 663000

CLOTHING

Stay warm

It is always colder on the sea than on land. Cold is a killer at sea. In water the human body loses heat 26 times quicker than in air.

Without special clothing, people are unlikely to survive more than 4 hours in water of 10°C. Many die within minutes of falling in.

goggles for personal watercraft and open powerboats

wear thermals underneath

Wet suit & dry suit

wet suit boots

WET SUIT   DRY SUIT

TIPS:
• *Wear plastic bags on your feet when putting on a wetsuit.*
• *Use candle wax to lubricate dry suit zips.*

A wet suit is suitable for immersion sports such as windsurfing, personal watercraft and high performance dinghy sailing in summer. Wetsuits trap a layer of water between the body and the suit.

A dry suit has seals at the neck and wrists and keeps the body and clothing dry. It is warmer than a wet suit and should be worn in open powerboats, personal watercraft and by dinghy sailors in cold weather. After zipping up, squeeze the air from a dry suit through the seals, or the trapped air may cause you to float ankles up. The most comfortable and most expensive dry suits are made of breathable material.

Foul-weather clothing

Yachtsmen and crew on motor cruisers need proper foul-weather clothing to keep dry and warm.

reflective tape

hood turns with head

large collar

handwarmer pockets

integral harness

bright colour

underneath wear thin thermals and fleecy middle layer

built-in buoyancy

waterproof gloves

tough patches

Foul-weather clothing

non-slip boots

TIP:
• *You can lose a lot of heat through your head – wear a hat.*

BUOYANCY AIDS AND LIFE-JACKETS

Wear:
- a buoyancy aid at all times in a sailing dinghy and on a personal watercraft
- a life-jacket at all times in an open powerboat and when going ashore in a yacht tender
- a life-jacket on a yacht or motor cruiser if you are a non-swimmer and when there is any possibility of entering the water
- a life-jacket when abandoning ship.

There are four types:

50N Buoyancy aid
This is suitable for dinghy sailing, personal watercraft and beginner windsurfers. It is an aid to swimming but will not self-right an unconscious person.

TIP:
• *Store your buoyancy aid on a hanger to drain the water after use.*

100N Buoyancy aid
More buoyant and usually with a floating collar. Suitable for competent swimmers and general inshore use, particularly for children, but will not self-right an unconscious person.

reflective tape

personal watercraft drivers have extra belts for strength

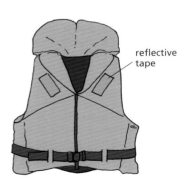

reflective tape

150N Life-jacket

This is the standard life-jacket recommended for offshore yachts, motor cruisers and open powerboats. When inflated, it will right an unconscious body and lift the mouth and nose above the water. It can be fitted with a light and some versions have a spray hood. Crutch straps prevent the jacket from riding up in the water.

Fit life-jackets as tight as you comfortably can.

TIP:
• *Inflate life-jackets regularly to check for leaks. Replace gas cylinders annually.*

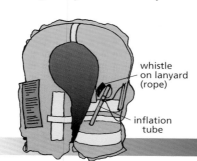

whistle on lanyard (rope)

inflation tube

150N Life-jacket

inflated 150N lifejacket

275N Life-jacket

This is for severe conditions and offshore workers carrying equipment. Unfortunately, they are bulky for small boat use.

Harness

A harness secures crew to the boat. Always wear one on motor cruisers and yachts at night, in rough weather, particularly when outside the cockpit, on the foredeck and at any time the skipper considers it necessary.

TIP:
• *Practise putting on your harness in port in daylight.*

Attach the harness to a strong point on the boat – jackstays (strong lines running the length of the deck) and d-rings. There should be an attachment point available for crew coming out of the companionway into the cockpit.

Harness

Always check the weather forecast before setting out to sea. You can obtain weather forecasts from:

• Harbour office
• Television
• Ceefax and teletext
• National radio
• Local radio (often the most accurate and relevant)
• Internet
• Telephone and fax services – Marine call (*see telephone directory*)
• Coastguard
• Navtex (electronic navigation and weather information system)

When listening to a forecast you need to take note of:

i. WIND DIRECTION
Wind causes waves. An offshore wind gives calm water inshore but you can get blown out to sea. An onshore wind gives a rougher sea inshore and blows you towards the land, which can be highly dangerous in a disabled boat. For dinghies and windsurfing, a wind along the beach is ideal.

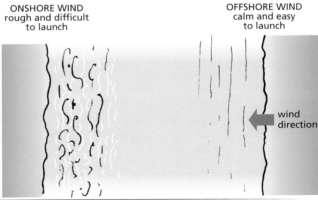

ONSHORE WIND
rough and difficult to launch

OFFSHORE WIND
calm and easy to launch

wind direction

Onshore and offshore winds

ii. WIND FORCE
See Beaufort wind scale on page 23.

iii. VISIBILITY
Fog can be dangerous.

Shipping forecast
Radio 4 LW at the following times – 0048, 0535 (0542 Sunday, 0556 Saturday), 1201, 1754. Coastguard marine VHF radio, every 4 hours on channels 10 and 73 after an announcement on channel 16.

WEATHER

Low pressure systems
Wind direction changes predictably as low pressure systems track across the UK. A typical system moves north east from the Atlantic Ocean.

TIP:
• Start learning about weather by identifying the cold front. It changes a drizzly south westerly wind into a bright and breezy north westerly.

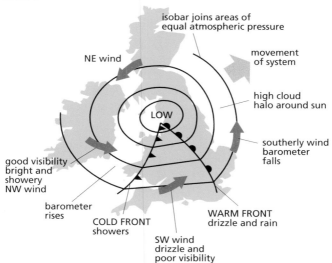

Low pressure system

High pressure systems
Move slowly and give settled weather.

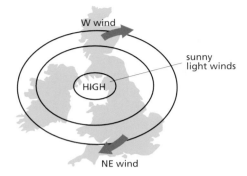

W wind

sunny
light winds

HIGH

NE wind

Sea breeze
In sunny weather the warm air rises above the land and cool air is drawn in from the sea. This causes an onshore sea breeze which lasts through the day but fades in the evening.

Fog is particularly hazardous. There are two types of fog:

i. RADIATION OR LAND FOG
Forms on land overnight in calm weather and drifts onto the sea. Is usually a problem in estuaries but often clears later in the day in the heat of the sun. Not found in open sea.

ii. ADVECTION OR SEA FOG
Is usually caused by warm air blowing over cold sea. Advection fog can occur at sea in strong winds and is cleared by a cold front.

TIP:
• The wind in harbour can be two forces less than outside.

BEAUFORT WIND SCALE

A 30 knot powerboat can be reduced to 5 knots in rough seas. As a rough guide, winds of force 5 and above are unsuitable for beginners in any craft.

Beaufort Wind Scale

Force	Wind Speed Knots	Description	Sea state	Probable wave height (m)
0	Less than 1	Calm	Sea like a mirror.	0
1	1-3	Light air	Ripples with the appearance of scales are formed but without foam.	0
2	4-6	Light breeze	Small wavelets, still short but more pronounced. Crests have a glassy appearance and do not break.	0.1
3	7-10	Gentle breeze	Large wavelets, crests begin to break; foam of glassy appearance, perhaps scattered white horses.	0.4
4	11-16	Moderate breeze	Small waves becoming longer; fairly frequent white horses.	1
5	17-21	Fresh breeze	Moderate waves taking a more pronounced long form; many white horses, chance of some spray.	2
6	22-27	Strong	Large waves begin to form and breezewhite foam crests become more extensive, probably some spray.	3
7	28-33	Near gale	Sea heaps up and white foam from the breaking waves begins to be blown in streaks.	4
8	34-40	Gale	Moderately high waves of greater length, edges of crests begin to break into spindrift. The foam blown in well-marked streaks.	5.5
9	41-47	Strong	High waves; dense streaks of foam. Crests begin to topple and roll over, spray may affect visibility.	7
10	48-55	Storm	Very high waves with long, overhanging crests. Foam in great patches is blown in dense white streaks making surface of the sea white. The tumbling of the sea becomes heavy and shock-like. Visibility is poor.	9
11	56-63	Violent	Exceptionally high waves; the sea is completely covered with patches of foam. Visibility is reduced.	11
12	64+	Hurricane	The air is filled with foam and spume; sea completely white with driving spray, visibility very seriously affected.	14

Nautical charts are available from chandlers' shops and specialised chart agents. Charts give detail of depth, land and sea marks, harbours and hazards.

Depths are measured in metres from a level called 'Chart Datum', corresponding to the lowest predicted tide which occurs every 10 years or so.

Heights are measured from 'Mean High Water Springs' which is an extra high tide level; *see page 28*.

Distances are measured in sea miles.
(1 sea mile = 1,852m)
There is a scale of miles on the side of the chart.

Specific symbols are used on charts.

Full details of all chart symbols are contained in the Admiralty publication Chart 5011, available from chandlers and chart agents.

You can record your position on the chart.
To find your position you can either use a visual method such as compass bearings or transits, or you can use the Global Positioning System (GPS).

TIP:
• Special packs of charts for small craft are available for certain popular areas.

map key:

 areas that cover and uncover

 red port buoy - marks left hand side of channel

 green starboard buoy - marks right hand side of channel

 26   depth 26m below chart datum

 drying rock

 wreck

 major light

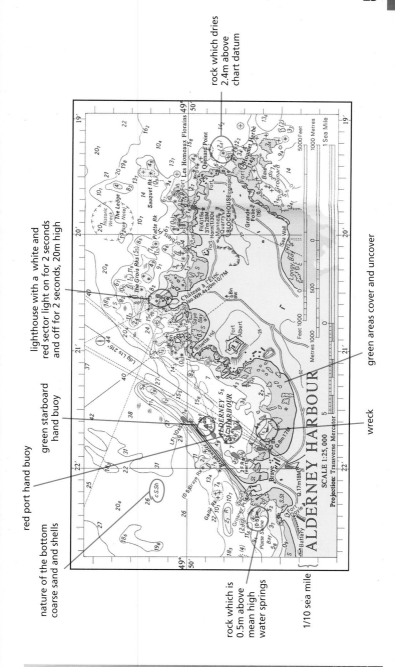

rock which dries 2.4m above chart datum

lighthouse with a white and red sector light on for 2 seconds and off for 2 seconds, 20m high

green starboard hand buoy

red port hand buoy

nature of the bottom coarse sand and shells

green areas cover and uncover

wreck

rock which is 0.5m above mean high water springs

ALDERNEY HARBOUR

SCALE 1:25,000

Projection: Transverse Mercator

1/10 sea mile

GPS is an accurate electronic means of obtaining
your position from satellite signals to a receiver on
your boat. GPS sets can be as small as a mobile
phone.

GPS

TIP:

• *GPS is a great
navigation
aid but it can
give you a
course over
land if wrongly
programmed.*

a GPS set can be programmed with
positions called waypoints and will
then read course and distance from
your position to the waypoint

When using GPS:

i. Keep a record of your position on the chart
    or in a log book.

ii. Confirm your position by another source
    e.g. visually or by echo sounder.

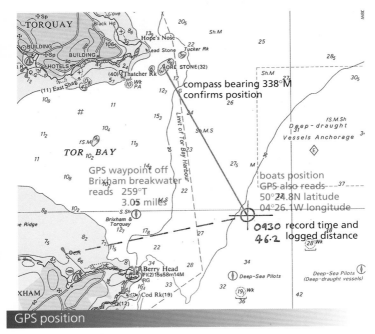

GPS position

A compass points towards Magnetic north (°M),
a few degrees different from True north (°T).

The chart will give the difference or variation. If the variation is, for example, 3° west, subtract this from a compass bearing to get the true bearing.

(a) Compass bearing 253° becomes true bearing 250°.

To convert a true bearing (say, a course on the chart) to a compass bearing with the same variation, add 3°.

(b) True bearing 026° becomes compass bearing 029°.

A steering compass on a boat can be affected by the ferrous metal around it giving an inaccuracy known as deviation. An expert, called a compass adjuster, can come on board and reduce this to a minimum and give you a deviation table of errors.

PLANNING CHECK-LIST

- Tell someone ashore where and when you are going and tell them when you get there.
- Plan destination and distance, and alternatives in case the weather deteriorates.
- Check weather.
- Times of high and low water.
- Tidal streams – find out strength and direction of change.
- Dangers – shipping channels, rocks, sandbanks etc.
- Harbour regulations – where you can and cannot launch and moor.
- Identify charted reference points ashore – lighthouses, conspicuous buildings etc.
- Take estimated fuel consumption + $1/3$.
- Food and water.
- Suitable clothing, life-jackets and buoyancy aids.
- Equipment, including radio.

Use the Coastguard CG66 scheme page 69. Complete this form with details of your craft and send it to the Coastguard. They will then have an accurate record in case of an emergency.

TIP:
• *Before you leave, stand on the beach with a chart and identify the main land and sea marks.*

TIDES

Tide tables can be purchased at chandlers' shops and chart agents. A tide table gives the times and heights of high and low water. Tidal heights are measured up from Chart Datum.

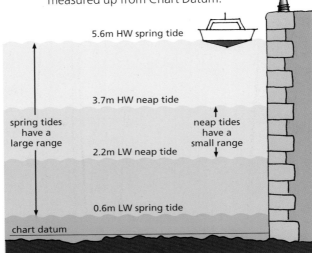

5.6m HW spring tide

3.7m HW neap tide

spring tides have a large range

neap tides have a small range

2.2m LW neap tide

0.6m LW spring tide

chart datum

Tide heights

most tables are written in GMT or UT - add one hour for British Summer Time

		time	m
spring tides	**TH 2**	0551	5.6 — high water
		1213	0.6 — low water
		1840	5.5

		time	m
neap tides one week later	**TH 9**	0021	3.7
		0645	2.2
		1301	3.7
		1920	2.1

TIPS:
• *Spring tides occur every two weeks at full moon and new moon.*
• *The time of high water is about one hour later each day.*

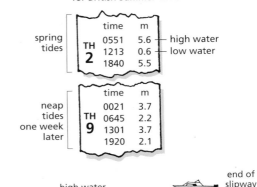

end of slipway

high water

drying rock

rock just below surface at low water

low water

deep channel

High & low water

The tide takes just over 6 hours to rise or to fall in most ports. The tide does not rise and fall evenly. It starts slowly and then increases its rate of change in the middle of the 6 hours and then slows down.

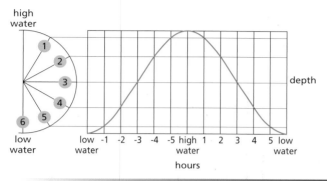

Rise & fall of tide

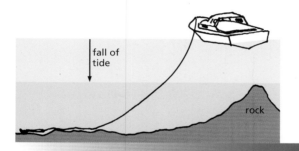

Fall of tide

Some areas such as the Solent have a 'stand'. The water stays high for 2 hours and then drops quickly over 5 hours.

Before mooring or anchoring your boat, you need to work out how much the tide will drop.

TIP:
• Always keep a record of the range of the tide. You will then know the total amount it will fall.

The movement of water along the coast is called the tidal stream. Tidal streams can be predicted using a tidal stream atlas or by referring to tables on a relevant chart.

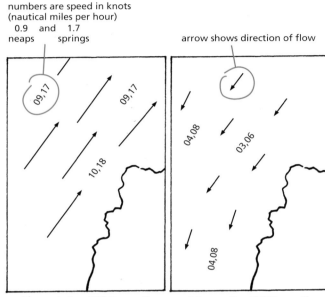

numbers are speed in knots
(nautical miles per hour)
  0.9   and   1.7
neaps   springs

arrow shows direction of flow

09,17

09,17

10,18

04,08

03,06

04,08

3 hours before HW Plymouth   **3 hours after HW Plymouth**

Tidal stream atlas

TIPS:
• *Keep a record of when the tidal stream changes.*
• *Use transits to sail across tidal streams.*

Tidal stream atlases can be purchased from chandlers' shops or chart agents. They give diagrams of the flow hour by hour, before or after high water at a reference port. The atlas usually has 12 chartlets, from 6 hours before to 6 hours after high water. If you know the time of high water, you can predict the tidal stream each hour.

The chart also gives tidal stream information. Magenta-lettered diamonds give the positions at which the tidal stream information is known hour by hour.

The tidal stream can be different near the coast in bays, near headlands, and over ledges.

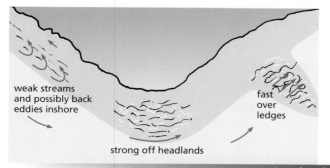

weak streams
and possibly back
eddies inshore

fast
over
ledges

strong off headlands

Local variations

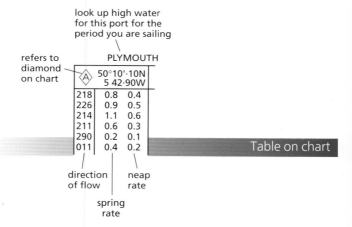

look up high water
for this port for the
period you are sailing

refers to
diamond
on chart

PLYMOUTH

◇A	50°10'·10N 5 42·90W	
218	0.8	0.4
226	0.9	0.5
214	1.1	0.6
211	0.6	0.3
290	0.2	0.1
011	0.4	0.2

Table on chart

direction
of flow

neap
rate

spring
rate

Tidal streams make a big difference to passage
times.

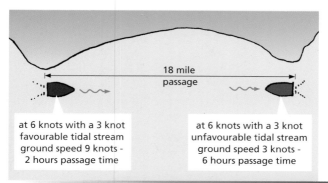

18 mile
passage

at 6 knots with a 3 knot
favourable tidal stream
ground speed 9 knots -
2 hours passage time

at 6 knots with a 3 knot
unfavourable tidal stream
ground speed 3 knots -
6 hours passage time

Tidal stream passage times

MARINE VHF RADIO

A VHF radio is the most useful method of communicating at sea. It puts you in direct touch with the Coastguard in an emergency and with other craft. You can also listen to weather forecasts and receive information about ship movements in harbour.

Before using a VHF radio

You need to pass a test to become an operator. This is called the Short Range Certificate and is run by the RYA. Contact them on 023 8062 7400 or www.rya.org.uk to find a course and assessment in your area.

The set needs to be licensed annually.

Contact:
Radio Licensing Centre, Post Office Customer Management, PO Box 1495, Bristol, BS99 3QS Telephone number – 0870 243 4433

The set has channels which are designated for specific purposes.

For example:

Channel	
6	Inter-ship
8	Inter-ship
12	Harbour and port operations
14	Harbour and port operations
16	Distress and calling
67	Coastguard
72	Inter-ship
77	Inter-ship
M	Marinas

TIP:
• If you need to call another boat, choose a channel in advance to avoid calling on channel 16.

Modern sets have Digital Selective Calling, DSC, which allows you to send digital messages, including distress calls on channel 70 which is exclusively for this purpose. Using this facility, part of the Global Maritime Distress and Safety System, GMDSS, the operator can inform the coastguard of the boat's position and nature of the emergency in a fraction of a second. It still allows you to give a conventional mayday message. *See page 65.*

4 hours, the coastguard broadcasts
ther information on channel 10 or
- nel 73. Times of these broadcasts are
  in the Nautical Almanac.
  tsmen should keep a listening watch on
  channel 16 for distress messages (you may be
able to help) and other announcements.
- In an emergency, the rescue services can home
  in on a VHF radio signal. They will ask you to
  transmit while their equipment identifies
  where you are.
- Mobile phones are useful to call numbers
  ashore but are much less effective at sea in an
  emergency because they do not allow you to
  talk to all stations, including the coastguard,
  simultaneously, and the rescue services cannot
  home in on them.
- Don't use the radio without training.
  There are certain procedures you must use
  to prevent chaos on the airwaves.
  For example:
     Say 'over' at the end of each transmission.
     Say 'out' at the end of work (not 'over and
     out').
     Take your finger off the transmit button to
     receive.
     Avoid channel 16 unless absolutely
     necessary or you may block out a distress
     call.

In busy areas such as the Solent, avoid using the
radio unless really necessary.

TIP:
*• Many radio
sets have
'dual watch' –
you can listen
to channel 16
and, say,
channel 67
simultaneously.*

COLLISION AVOIDANCE

Nearly all collisions at sea are caused by one or more people not keeping a good lookout. This is as true for supertankers as it is for jet skis.

TIPS:
• *Don't forget to look behind you.*
• *If the compass bearing of the other boat doesn't change, you're on a collision course.*

Powered craft or yachts under power

Change course early and obviously.

CROSSING SITUATION

this craft which has the other on its right or starboard side gives way - "give way to the right"

HEAD ON

both turn to starboard

OVERTAKING

overtaking boat keeps clear

powerboats give way to sailing craft additionally powerboats give way to: fishing boats which display shape –

dredgers which display –

pass this side of the diamonds

and keep clear of tugs and tows which show – if the tow is over 200m

Power craft give way to sailing craft

A collision between most small craft is often expensive but rarely life-threatening, except for personal watercraft where it is the main cause of fatalities.

Sailing vessels

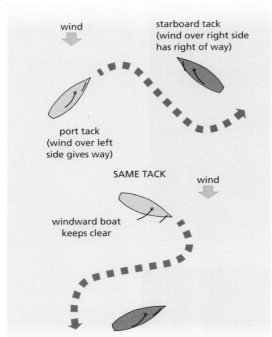

CROSSING

wind

starboard tack
(wind over right side
has right of way)

port tack
(wind over left
side gives way)

SAME TACK

wind

windward boat
keeps clear

IF IN DOUBT...

wind

...KEEP CLEAR!

sailing boats give way to:
dredgers
fishing boats
and keep clear of tugs
and tows

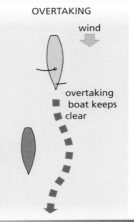

OVERTAKING

wind

overtaking
boat keeps
clear

TIPS:
- *Keep a good lookout under the sail – particularly on port tack.*
- *If you suspect the other boat has not seen you – give way.*

COLLISION AVOIDANCE AT NIGHT

TIPS:
• Keep clear of ships in harbour and narrow channels.
• Avoid getting into a situation where a ship has to take avoiding action.

red and green sidelights a white steaming light and a white stern light

At night, a powerboat under 50m shows:

• red and green sidelights

• a white steaming light

• a white stern light.

Powerboat under 50m

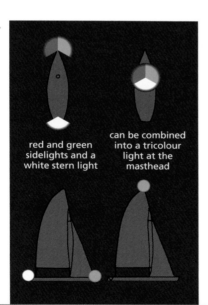

red and green sidelights and a white stern light

can be combined into a tricolour light at the masthead

At night, a sailing yacht shows:

• red and green sidelights
  and
• a white stern light
  or
• can be combined into a tricolour light at the masthead.

Sailing yacht

At night, a ship over 50m shows:

- red and green sidelights
- a white stern light
- two white steaming lights.

two white steaming lights
red and green sidelights and
a white sternlight

Ship over 50m

At night, a small power vessel under 7m and speed under 7 knots shows:

- all round white light.

all round white light

Small power vessel under 7m

At night, when a yacht is motoring, it should show the lights of a power vessel.

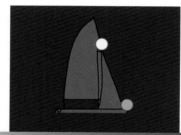

Yacht motoring

At night, be particularly careful of:

Tugs and tows
A vessel towing shows:

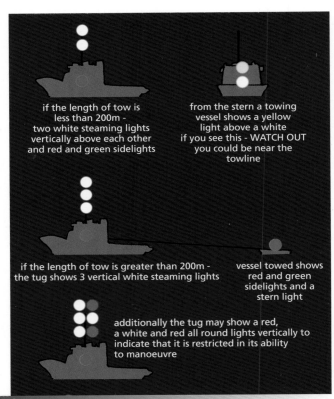

if the length of tow is less than 200m - two white steaming lights vertically above each other and red and green sidelights

from the stern a towing vessel shows a yellow light above a white if you see this - WATCH OUT you could be near the towline

if the length of tow is greater than 200m - the tug shows 3 vertical white steaming lights

vessel towed shows red and green sidelights and a stern light

additionally the tug may show a red, a white and red all round lights vertically to indicate that it is restricted in its ability to manoeuvre

Tugs & tows

TIP:
• Remember the lights of the tug and trawler, and don't go close to their sterns.

Fishing boats

fishing boats show all round red over an all round white on the mast

BEWARE OF TRAWLERS they show an all round green over an all round white on the mast **DON'T PASS CLOSE TO THE STERN**

Fishing boats

Other ships that both yachts and small powerboats should avoid are:

- Vessels not under command (cannot take avoiding action)

shows:

in daylight

at night

Vessels not under command

- Vessels restricted in ability to manoeuvre

shows:

in daylight

at night

Vessels restricted in ability to manoeuvre

when entering a harbour buoys and beacons
will appear red to port and green to starboard

the cardinal system which
indicates dangerous areas
is based on the points
of a compass

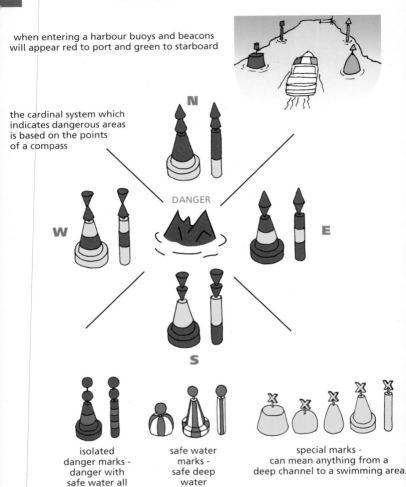

N

DANGER

W   E

S

isolated
danger marks -
danger with
safe water all
around

safe water
marks -
safe deep
water

special marks -
can mean anything from a
deep channel to a swimming area

Types of buoys

TIP:
• *The colours
on a cardinal
buoy match
the top mark.
The points
of the cone
point towards
the black.*

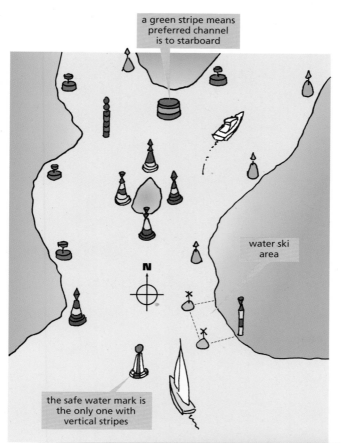

a green stripe means
preferred channel
is to starboard

water ski
area

the safe water mark is
the only one with
vertical stripes

Buoy channel

TIPS:
• You can
see cardinal
marks from
approximately
2 miles away.
• The safewater
mark is the
only one with
vertical stripes.

TIPS:
- *Ships make sound signals when manoeuvring*
  1 blast turning to starboard
  2 blasts turning to port
  3 blasts going astern.
- *If the visibility is poor, you are much safer in shallow water.*

Recreational craft can successfully share harbours with commercial shipping, providing everyone knows the rules.

Many harbours produce guides for small craft. They are available from the harbour master or local marinas and chandlers.

Zones for personal watercraft, water-skiing and windsurfing are usually marked with yellow buoys.

You will probably need permission to launch and will probably have to pay.

Some harbours have a registration scheme for personal watercraft.

Most harbours have a speed limit.

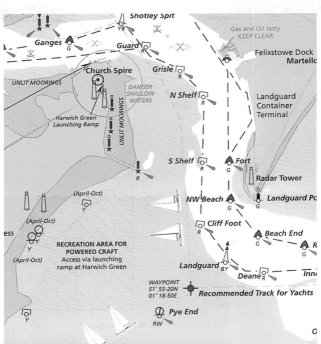

Harwich guide

A small boat may not be visible from the bridge of a large ship.

Small boats may not be visible from ships

Remember, ships have to keep to the main channels and they often cannot stop or alter course to avoid small craft.

Keep outside shipping channels

- If possible keep outside the buoyed shipping channels.
- Listen to the port operations channel on the VHF radio for shipping movements. Don't speak on it unless you need to contact the harbour master urgently.
- Cross shipping channels quickly and at right angles.
- In some ports, you are forbidden to enter certain areas when ships are manoeuvring.
- Keep clear of commercial docks.
- Some parts of the harbour may be designated as quiet or conservation areas. Take particular care to keep noise and speed down in these areas.

TIP:
• In some harbours, a harbour launch leads ships in. Don't go between the launch and the ship.

PILOTAGE

Pilotage is the skill of navigating in harbours and close to the land. It is usually easier to do this visually rather than rely on GPS.

- Prepare a plan for entering or leaving a harbour. Draw it on a chart (laminated for open boats).
- Draw courses and distances on the chart.
- For powerboats you may wish to record approximate times of arrival.

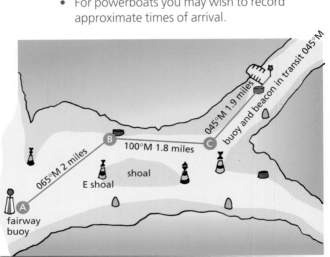

Plan for entering a harbour

A. Check with compass to identify correct red buoy.
B. Turn when well past E shoal buoy.
C. Look out for transit. Check it is correct with compass.

- If you get lost, go back to a known position. With a compass and a chart, you should be able to identify the next mark.
- Tick off the buoys as you pass them.

Common mistakes in pilotage

- Misidentifying buoys – check the next buoy with a compass from a known position.
- Allowing the tidal stream to drift the boat off track – steer on transits.
- Running aground – check the tidal height.

TIP:
• If the harbour is shallow and unknown to you, enter on a rising tide.

Transits

Transits can give you a position line to the
accuracy of a boat length. Many harbours have
transits to take you into the entrance.

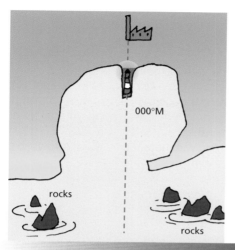

000°M

rocks

rocks

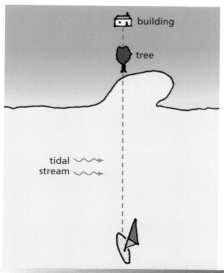

building

tree

tidal
stream

- Always check a charted transit with a compass
  – you might be lining up the wrong objects.
- Transits can be used by all types of craft to
  ensure you are crossing the tidal stream by the
  most direct route.

CAPSIZE

Dinghies

Modern dinghies can be recovered very quickly from a capsize. Once upright they normally drain without the use of a bailer.

If you capsize:

- Stay with the boat.
- Helm climbs over or swims to the centreboard and stands on it. Hold to prevent the boat inverting. When swimming, you can use the mainsheet as a safety line.
- Crew swims into the boat and throws jib sheet to helmsman.

Recovery of dinghy capsize

TIP:
• Be careful not to climb up the hull on the inside – you could invert the dinghy, possibly damaging the mast on the sea bed.

- Crew lies in water next to hull while helm stands on centreboard, holds the jib sheet and leans back.
- As boat rights, crew is scooped in.

Personal watercraft

This is a regular part of personal watercraft driving. Personal watercraft are designed to be recovered from capsize.

- Stay with the craft.
- You must wear a kill cord or the personal watercraft will not stop when you fall off it. You could also injure your fingers by putting them in the water intake if the engine is running.
- The stern of a personal watercraft has a label which indicates which way to rotate the machine to bring it upright.

CAUTION!

TO AVOID POSSIBLE ENGINE FLOODING WHEN ROLLING OVER:

- **MAKE SURE ENGINE IS OFF**
- **GRAB INLET GRATE AND STEP ON BUMPER RAIL**
- **ROLL BOAT CLOCKWISE**

TIP:
- *If the engine will not start, it may be flooded. Leave it a short while and try again. Don't try to open the engine compartment at sea – you could capsize and sink.*

Rotating the craft

- Swim alongside, put one hand on the intake grill and one on the grab handle and roll the craft over.
- Climb over the stern, taking care not to step on any jet parts.
- Reattach the kill cord and start without choke.
- If you are carrying a passenger, the driver climbs aboard first.

Calling for help

Only call for help if you have done everything to try to self-rescue. The Royal National Lifeboat Institution (RNLI) is not a 'tow you home' service, they save lives. It is safer, particularly in small powerboats and personal watercraft, to operate a buddy system so you can be towed home if necessary. Keep a towline on board.

The simplest way of calling for help is to move your arms up and down at the side.

Calling for help

A VHF radiotelephone, particularly on digital selective calling, puts you instantly in touch with the coastguard or other craft. *See page 32*.

A mobile phone puts you in touch with a land operator who can put you through to a coastguard. The rescue service will not be able to home in on its signal and you will not be able to talk to a lifeboat or rescue helicopter as you can with a VHF radio.

An Emergency Position Indicating Radio Beacon, EPIRB, when activated, informs rescue services of your position and the nature of your distress. It must be registered with the coastguard so they have a record of your boat.

Register EPIRBs with:
    EPIRB Register
    MRCC Falmouth
    Pendennis Point
    Castle Drive
    Falmouth
    TR11 4WZ

TIP:
• If a rescue craft or helicopter is looking for you, you can signal to them with a mirror in sunlight.

All craft on the sea, except those attended by rescue or safety boats, should carry distress flares to attract attention in an emergency.

Read the instructions in daylight when you purchase them. Don't wait for an emergency.

Distress flares are red or orange and there are three main types:

TIPS:
• Fire flares in groups of two – they are more likely to be seen than one.
• Flares can become out of date. Check the expiry date and replace if necessary.

Hand-held red pinpoint

Visible for 7 miles on a clear night or about 5 miles by day. Useful when you can see a lifeboat or rescue helicopter looking for you. There are different types with different ignition systems.

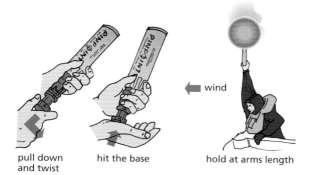

pull down and twist   hit the base   wind   hold at arms length

Hand-held red pinpoint flares

- Hold downwind.
- Don't look at the flare once it is ignited.
- Take care to hold by the handle – the barrel gets red hot.

Orange smoke

Can be seen for 3 miles in daylight. Useful for rescue helicopters to identify your position and also assess wind direction.

- Always ignite downwind. The smoke is acrid.

Buoyant orange smoke

Parachute rockets

Can be seen for 25 miles in good visibility.
The flare rises to about 300m and then falls
slowly under a parachute.

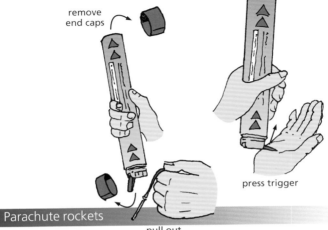

remove
end caps

press trigger

Parachute rockets

pull out
safety pin

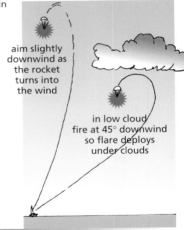

aim slightly
downwind as
the rocket
turns into
the wind

in low cloud
fire at 45° downwind
so flare deploys
under clouds

Aiming parachute rockets

Mini-flares are small red rockets which only last
a short time but are light and easy to carry.

Day/night flares combine a red pinpoint at one
end and orange smoke at the other. They are
compact and suitable for personal watercraft
and other small craft.

Don't underestimate the seriousness of this.
Cold water rapidly saps your strength.
The sooner the boat gets back, the easier the
recovery out of the water. It is very difficult
to retrieve unconscious people.

Powerboats

Always wear a kill cord. There have been several
fatalities caused by drivers falling out and the
unmanned powerboat circling around and
passing over a person in the water.

If a crew member falls out:

TIP:
*• Take great
care not to
allow the
propeller
anywhere
near someone
in the water.*

- If you still have crew in the boat, they should
  point at the person in the water while you
  make a U-turn back to the casualty.

- Approach from downwind, aiming just off
  to one side.

- Use gentle astern power if necessary to stop
  the boat, with the casualty in front of the helm
  position.

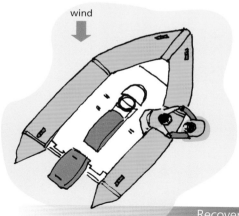

wind

Recovery of man overboard

- At the same time, turn the boat so that it is at
  a slight angle to the wind, with the casualty on
  the downwind side.

- Make sure the engine is out of gear.

Motor cruisers

In a motor cruiser, there is no ideal system

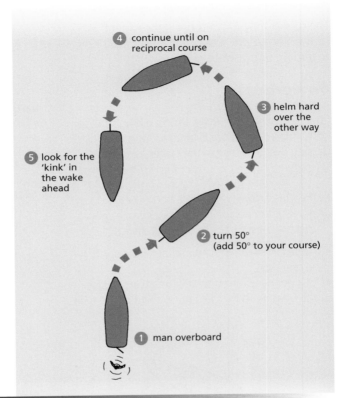

4 continue until on reciprocal course

3 helm hard over the other way

5 look for the 'kink' in the wake ahead

2 turn 50° (add 50° to your course)

1 man overboard

Returning to casualty

TIP:
• *If you are not sure of your boat-handling skills, make contact with a long floating line but mind the propeller.*

Approach about 10ft off to windward on the helmsman side.

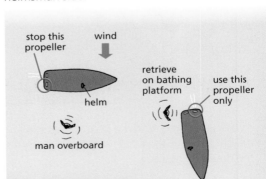

stop this propeller

wind

helm

retrieve on bathing platform

use this propeller only

man overboard

Stop the propeller on the side of the casualty

Yachts

The first action is to shout 'man overboard' and allocate a crew member to point.

Stop the boat by tacking with the jib cleated into the heave-to position. There are many methods of returning but the two most common are:

i. QUICK STOP

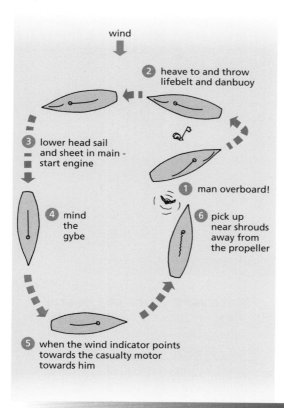

wind

2 heave to and throw lifebelt and danbuoy

3 lower head sail and sheet in main - start engine

1 man overboard!

4 mind the gybe

6 pick up near shrouds away from the propeller

5 when the wind indicator points towards the casualty motor towards him

Quick stop

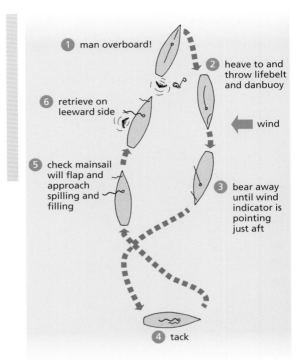

1 man overboard!

2 heave to and throw lifebelt and danbuoy

wind

6 retrieve on leeward side

5 check mainsail will flap and approach spilling and filling

3 bear away until wind indicator is pointing just aft

4 tack

Reach-tack-reach

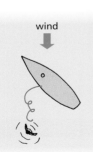

wind

Throwing a line downwind

Recovery from the water

Pulling people out of the water is difficult, especially if they are weak and cold.

Throw a floating line to make contact. It is very difficult to throw a line into the wind, so position the boat with the casualty downwind.

In calm weather, the casualty, if conscious, will be able to climb up the boarding ladder or bathing platform.

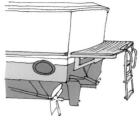

Boarding ladder & bathing platform

In rough weather, it may be necessary to retrieve them with a block and tackle. Many yachts have a detachable mainsheet which can be adapted to pull people out of the water using the boom as a crane.

Block & tackle

You can also use a half-inflated dinghy alongside a yacht.

Think about this problem before it happens and work out a system for your boat.

TIP:
• *Try to get a line around the casualty as soon as you can.*

Half-inflated dinghy

Surviving in the water

If you are unlucky enough to fall into the water, you will survive longer if you:

- Are wearing a life-jacket.
- Have several layers of clothing to keep warm.
- Don't try to swim unless help is close by.
- Conserve heat in the HELP position.

**HEAT ESCAPE
LESSENING POSTURE**

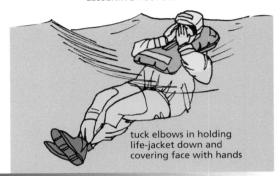

tuck elbows in holding
life-jacket down and
covering face with hands

Heat escape lessening posture

TIP:
• You stand a much better chance of survival if you conserve heat and stay determined and positive – believe you will be rescued!

Unfortunately, if it is windy, your legs act as a drogue which turns your face into the wind.

Try to protect your mouth and nose from the spray. A spray hood is ideal.

Spray hood

To learn how to use a life-raft, attend a RYA one-day Sea Survival Course. This gives you a chance to practice using the equipment in a swimming pool.

Life-rafts should be stowed either:

i. in a canister on deck
ii. in a dedicated locker, opening into the cockpit.

Hydrostatic release unit

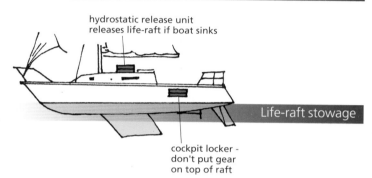

hydrostatic release unit
releases life-raft if boat sinks

Life-raft stowage

cockpit locker -
don't put gear
on top of raft

Life-rafts have a painter, which you pull to inflate. The painter should be attached to a strong point on the boat. To launch, throw the raft over the leeward side and pull the painter. Keep the raft close to the boat. Only launch the life-raft if you really have to. The boat is a better life-raft, even if it is disabled. Send a distress call.

TIP:
• *Put the strongest and heaviest person in the raft first to stabilise it and help the others in.*

Life-raft launch

If you have to abandon ship, make every effort to stay dry. It is difficult to enter rafts from the water.

Once in a life-raft, there are 4 initial actions:

cut, stream, close, maintain.

CUT the painter to get clear of the boat.

STREAM the drogue. This stabilises the raft and keeps it in position.

CLOSE shut the raft entrance to keep out spray and stay warm inside.

MAINTAIN the security of the raft by checking for leaks and bail out.

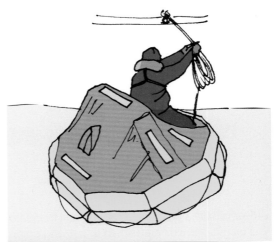

Cut the painter

Stream the drogue

TIP:
• *Nearly everyone feels seasick in a raft – take anti-seasickness tablets.*

Find out the contents of your raft when you purchase or hire it. Many do not include food.

BOAT HANDLING

The best way to learn boat handling is to go on a course.

There are some basic principles that apply to all craft.

Power

Approach alongside berths and moorings into the tidal stream.

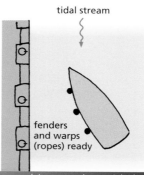

tidal stream

fenders and warps (ropes) ready

Approaching an alongside berth

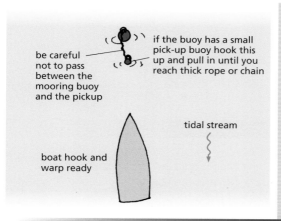

be careful not to pass between the mooring buoy and the pickup

if the buoy has a small pick-up buoy hook this up and pull in until you reach thick rope or chain

tidal stream

boat hook and warp ready

Approaching a mooring

TIPS:

• *Communicate clearly with the crew. Don't say 'OK on the bow' – give instruction 'let go of the mooring'.*

• *The direction of moored boats and the flow of water on moorings and posts will indicate the direction of the tidal stream.*

Leave into the tidal stream also, even if it means going out astern.

Practice on a berth with plenty of room.

Find out the difference between berthing with the wind blowing onto the pontoon (easy to berth, hard to get off) and wind blowing off the pontoon (hard to berth, easy to get off).

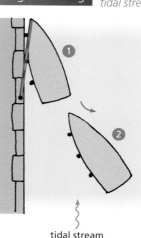

doubling your bowline back as a spring will allow the stern to come out

tidal stream

Leaving an alongside berth

Sail

To slow the boat down, sail on a close reach.
Approach moorings this way when wind and
tidal stream are in the same direction.

A close reach is also useful for approaching
a man overboard and for reefing.

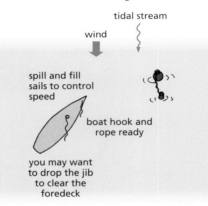

Mooring with the wind and tide in the same direction

If the wind is opposed to the tide, approach
moorings into the tide under jib alone. This also
works if the wind is across the tide.

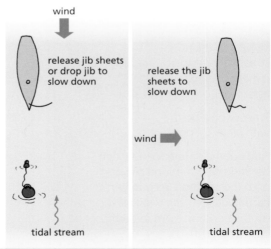

Mooring when wind and tide are opposed or across stream

- Keep clear of bathers.
- Be considerate to other water users such as fishermen and anglers. Keep your distance and go slow.
- Never take out any craft when intoxicated.
- Keep noise down
    i. in marinas and near moorings
    ii. in conservation areas
    iii. close to shore.
- Keep your distance from other craft, especially ships.
- Keep clear of yacht, dinghy and powerboat races.
- Don't disturb wildlife such as dolphins and seals.
- Keep your craft in good order. Don't become a lifeboat statistic.
- Keep an eye on the weather – if it's deteriorating, return to shore.
- Practise emergency procedures such as man overboard. Good boat handlers are safer.
- If sailing, avoid getting downwind and down tide of your destination.
- Stay warm. Cold kills.
- Always keep track of your position. Don't get lost.
- Keep a good lookout.
- Don't get dehydrated. Take water with you.
- Have an alternative plan for bad weather.
- Brief your crew – they need to know.

- There are specific rules for the use of boat trailers.
- Speed limits are 60mph on dual carriageways and motorways, and 50mph on other roads. There are limits on the size and weight of trailers, condition of brakes and tyres, lights and markings.
- Check whether your driving licence allows you to tow. New drivers may have to take an extra test.

Before you launch

- Allow the wheel bearings to cool before launching.
- Check that the boat is ready, fuel, bungs, equipment, kill cord etc.
- Reverse carefully down the slipway. Watch out for swimmers and obstructions.
- To avoid possible damage to the car, on shallow slipways lower the jockey wheel on the trailer and use a rope from the tow bar.

Float the boat off when launching.

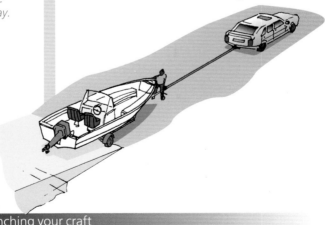

Launching your craft

Personal watercraft

Start the engine for a few seconds to check it
works before launching.

Recovery

- You may have to tie the craft near the slipway
  while you reverse the trailer into the water.
- Cut the engine in a metre of water to avoid
  damage, and drift in.
- You may have to stand in the water.

Recovery

- Winch the craft onto the trailer.
- Make sure the winch is locked before driving
  up the slip.
- Wash down with fresh water. If you are not
  using the craft regularly, then flush the engine
  cooling system with fresh water.
- Strap on securely.
- Attach light board.

TIP:

- *Plug in the
trailer board
and lay it
down beside
the car to
check that
the lights and
indicators
work.*

DID YOU KNOW?

1. RYA training schemes are respected and emulated throughout the world.
2. There are practical RYA courses on every aspect of boating from jet skis, through powerboats, to offshore yachting, from dinghy sailing for children to advanced windsurfing techniques.
3. There are RYA shore-based courses which you can attend for one day on diesel engines, sea survival, first aid, radar and marine VHF radio.
4. When you successfully complete a course, you are awarded an RYA certificate.
5. The RYA runs examinations for the Maritime and Coastguard Agency for yachtmaster and coastal skipper and provides commercial certificates for professional skippers.
6. The RYA authorises test centres for the International Certificate of Competence.
7. RYA Instructors are all qualified practically – they must know the subject and demonstrate teaching technique.
8. The RYA regularly inspects all practical schools.
9. Over 120,000 people completed RYA courses at 1,500 centres last year.

MAYDAY CALL

A mayday call is the equivalent of dialing 999 and may only be sent when there is 'grave and imminent danger to the vessel or person'.

SWITCH ON VHF RADIO SET
TURN TO CHANNEL 16
USE HIGH POWER
PRESS TRANSMIT BUTTON AND SAY:

MAYDAY MAYDAY MAYDAY

THIS IS (NAME OF VESSEL, NAME OF VESSEL, NAME OF VESSEL)

MAYDAY (NAME OF VESSEL)

MY POSITION IS (LATITUDE AND LONGITUDE, OR BEARING AND DISTANCE FROM A FIXED OBJECT)

TYPE OF DISTRESS (ON FIRE, HOLED AND SINKING, ETC)

I REQUIRE IMMEDIATE ASSISTANCE

I HAVE (NUMBER) OF PEOPLE ON BOARD

ANY OTHER INFORMATION
(E.G. ABANDONING TO LIFE-RAFT)

OVER

RELEASE TRANSMIT BUTTON AND WAIT FOR REPLY

HOW TO JOIN THE SAFETY IDENTIFICATION SCHEME

IT'S FREE AND COULD SAVE YOUR LIFE

- Complete the enclosed Safety Identification Scheme (CG66) questionnaire in ink and send it to the nearest Coastguard Co-ordination Centre.

- Enclose a recent photograph of your craft, if you have one.

- In return you will be sent an information pack containing details of other safety information and registration schemes, and a card with brief details for your shore contact. This gives instructions on what action to take should they be concerned for the safety of the vessel/craft.

- This information will be entered on to a database and will be available to all Coastguard Co-ordination Centres. Its purpose will be to provide HM Coastguard with up-to-date details of the vessel/craft in a search and rescue situation and the provision of safety information.

- You will also be provided with a change of details card.

- If you change the name of the craft or any address given on the form, you should complete the card and return it to your Coastguard Co-ordination Centre .

- You should also return the card if the craft's appearance changes (colour etc), if there is any significant change to the equipment held, or if you are no longer the owner.

- The Safety Identification Card is valid for two years. If it is not renewed within that time, it will be considered invalid and removed from the records.

Maritime and Coastguard Agency

COASTGUARD MARITIME CO-ORDINATION CENTRES

MRCC Aberdeen
Marine House,
Blaikies Quay,
Aberdeen,
AB1 2PB
Tel: 01224 592334

MRSC Belfast
Bregenz House,
Quay Street,
Bangor,
BT20 5ED
Tel: 01247 463933

MRSC Brixham
Kings Quay,
Brixham,
Devon,
TQ5 9TW
Tel: 01803 882704

MRCC Clyde
Navy Buildings,
Eldon Street,
Greenock,
PA16 7QY
Tel: 01475 729988

MRCC Dover
Langdon Battery,
Swingate,
Dover,
Kent,
CT15 5NA
Tel: 01304 210008

MRCC Falmouth
Pendennis Point,
Castle Drive,
Falmouth,
Cornwall,
TR11 4WZ
Tel: 01326 317575

MRSC Holyhead
Prince of Wales Road,
Holyhead,
Anglesey,
North Wales,
LL65 1ET
Tel: 01407 762051/
763911

MRSC Humber
Lime Kiln Lane,
Bridlington,
East Yorkshire,
YO15 2LX
Tel: 01262 672317

MRSC Liverpool
Hall Road West,
Crosby,
Liverpool,
L23 8SY
Tel: 0151 931 3341

MRSC Milford Haven
Gorsewood Drive,
Hakin,
Milford Haven,
Pembrokeshire,
SA73 3ER
Tel: 01646 690909

MRSC Pentland
Fifeness,
Crail,
Fife,
KY10 3XN
Tel: 01333 450666

MRSC Portland
Custom House Quay,
Weymouth,
Dorset,
DT4 8BE
Tel: 01305 760439

MRSC Shetland
The Knab,
Knab Road,
Lerwick,
Shetland,
ZE1 OAX
Tel: 01595 692976

MRSC Solent
Whyecroft House,
44 Marine Parade West,
Lee on Solent,
Hampshire,
PO13 9WR
Tel: 02392 552100

MRSC Stornoway
Battery Point,
Stornoway,
Isle of Lewis,
HS1 2RT
Tel: 01851 702013/
702014

MRCC Swansea
Tutt Head,
Mumbles,
Swansea,
SA3 4EX
Tel: 01792 366534

MRSC Thames
East Terrace,
Walton-on-Naze,
Essex,
CO14 8PY
Tel: 01255 675518

MRCC Yarmouth
Havenbridge House,
4th Floor,
Great Yarmouth,
NR30 1HZ
Tel: 01493 851339

Maritime and Coastguard Agency

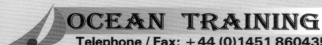

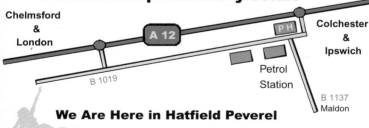